# Love Letters to the 305

## A COLLECTION OF MIAMI
## POETRY & PHOTOGRAPHY

Cover Art Copyright © 2023 by Indie Earth Publishing

Edited by Flor Ana Mireles

1st Edition | 01
Paperback ISBN: 979-8-9869891-7-4

First Published March 2023

For inquiries and bulk orders, please email:
indieearthpublishinghouse@gmail.com

Printed in the United States

1 2 3 4 5 6 7 8 9


Indie Earth Publishing Inc.
| Miami, FL |

INDIE EARTH
PUBLISHING

# LOVE LETTERS TO THE 305

# Contents

*"Almost everything strange washes up near Miami."*
*- Rick Riordan*

*"Miami, you can never run out of material. As long as you have Miami around you, you will never, never stop being amused."*
*- Dave Barry*

*For Miami, our beautiful city*

## *Advice for a Tourist*
Micah Marie Johnson

South Beach?
For some reason
Everyone is in a hurry.
Haven't you heard of
Miami Time,
The vortex of
Mañana, mañana?
The move real slow
Until everything arrives.

We live where you vacation.

Maybe it's hard to notice
That everything is different.
All our friends moved away
And threaten they won't come back
For the cafecito
Or the weather.
The endless sky fills,
Structures threatening to scrape.

We are always on the way to reinvention.

Some buildings take a lifetime,
Built to be left empty.
Some parts of the city are so full
People just stay indoors
Avoiding the heat.
Laughing at traffic,
Guiding and lamenting:
"Don't drive here."

We won't meet you anywhere on time.

This is the beach.
This is transient.
This is home, but not Miami.
This is your last chance to see it this way.
Take the picture.
Take the hint.
Take the trolley.
Take the city in strides.

### 305

Luis Fernando

Miami, city of endless heat,
Where the sun shines bright and bold,
A melting pot of cultures and beats,
Where traditions are never sold.

Cuban coffee, a daily treat,
For those who crave its bold and rich flavor,
A reminder of the island's soul,
A taste of home for those who labor.

In Miami, Latino diversity thrives,
A tapestry of cultures and traditions,
Where salsa and cumbia music vibe,
And the vibrant art scene never dulls.

Beaches of crystal blue,
Are the city's shining crown,
Where tourists flock to soak up the sun,
And locals gather to unwind and drown.

Miami, a city of endless fun,
A true reflection of Latino spirit and soul,
A place to experience the best of culture,
In this vibrant and colorful metropolis, our home.

# Sunsets in Bloom

*Amalia Maria*

## *Miami Protest Song*
Renzo Del Castillo

Outside, another storm.
Our sky, the color of rotten peaches, rains stones,
mercilessly bombarding the bird droppings
adorning the roof of my mother's Mazda.

I don't recognize anything.
I have forgotten how to speak the language of this house.
I'm considering hiring a translator so I can ask for permission.
I'm uncomfortable using the bathroom
but I take my liberties with the liquor cabinet.

Whole wheat bread and white cheese
are my faithful companions when night and day fuck,
entangled in a colossal Kama Sutra.

The internet provides loans to survive this melatonin bankruptcy;
but, like any son of a bitch,
it raises the interest rate while I'm distracted.
My wallet is empty, nonetheless,
I feel its weight hindering my steps.

Everything is expensive; even meditation costs time.
What do you expect in a city where Nag Champa is used to disguise
the stench of blunts?

I can imagine Jesus playing Monopoly
with Buddha, Jehovah, Ja, Allah, and the Sun,
laughing as he passes "Go" and receives an additional $25 for his services
when his token ends up in the Community Chest.

The whole group drinking Chilean wine,
sitting on marshmallow clouds, taking the day off;

sick of the office's water cooler talk, hearing how we commit atrocities
in their name
when they have nothing to do with it.

And down here,
loneliness tastes of cheap vodka and cinnamon tea.

## **Birthday Stroll**

*Petit Monstre*

### *Acrónimo*
Flor Ana

Flowers dance all around me in a
Room of coladas and cortaditos while
Everyone sings their Celia Cruz and
Eats the delicacies of a land only 90 miles away.


Casually, we bring up 'good old days' & wonder just how good they were
Under a dictatorship that never cared for the people anyway.
But, one day, i'll see my motherland again,
And we'll dance and sway our hips together among the stars

*Para Miami*

*and i'll be grateful that Miami never let me forget my roots...*

### *Bustelo*
Luis Fernando

Miami, city of heat and hue
Cuban coffee, a daily treat
Latino culture, shining bright

## *My heart*
Rebekah Malkin

Broken winged fireflies
Sputter in a vacant field
Where blossoms cannot bloom
Grasses stand still
In the swaying winds
Dandelions left spur-less
Winds don't cry home
Laying heavily
Restless
Over our caved in chests
Hills hang low
Shattered from the absence
Of half filled promises
"I'll see you there"

# *La Ciudad X29*

*Para Miami*

*Rafael Guillen*

## *Fast girls (in the early 00's)*
Erin Sternstein


Fast Girls skip meals like classes
Fill their bras with paper napkins
sneak out windows like it's their passion.
Puffing Black and Milds as they crowd surf at The Pit

Fast girls stick out their tongue in photos
Taste buds stained by bright blue Blow Pops.
Practicing blow jobs in parking lots.
Fast Girls sexuality is performatively Bi.

Fast Girls use FarmStores to buy Smirnoff ice for the boy in the black
BMW with black windows, black pants, and a single chain around his
neck.

Daddy Yankee blasts through his speakers
The gel in his hair forms a tower of spikes.
His arms are shaved like his fast girl in the front seat.

Fast Girls plan sleepovers using a friend's name so they can sleep at a boys
house because college boyfriends in Freshman year of high school are to
be kept a secret and—
"It isn't like weird, right?"

When Fast girls do share it's because shame catches them.
And only then do they tell you that they use your name
And only then do they say things like please and "come with me to his
place."
And your hand tremors as you agree.

So, you get to his place
The boy and the fast girl leave.
You don't know if she got confident or he got bold.

His friend waits patiently on the couch, sharpening his teeth like knives.

How many years did fast girls talk you into unwanted sexual situations so that you can live up to their definition of a "good friend"

Peer pressure only exists in spaces where you believe you are equals.

And you learn.

In these days before Columbine, razor blades pass through hallways like chewing gum and pregnancy tests- so many girls practicing a pain that would come later

And you learn.

And you shave arm hair and stomach in Biology class.

And you practice.

Sun-ripened raspberry sprinkled on each follicle.

And you remember how the razor felt in your hand, how the blade pressed into the skin.

Hair grew in different directions then, yet each one
wanted so much to belong.

# *The Boombox*

*Sofia Iriarte*

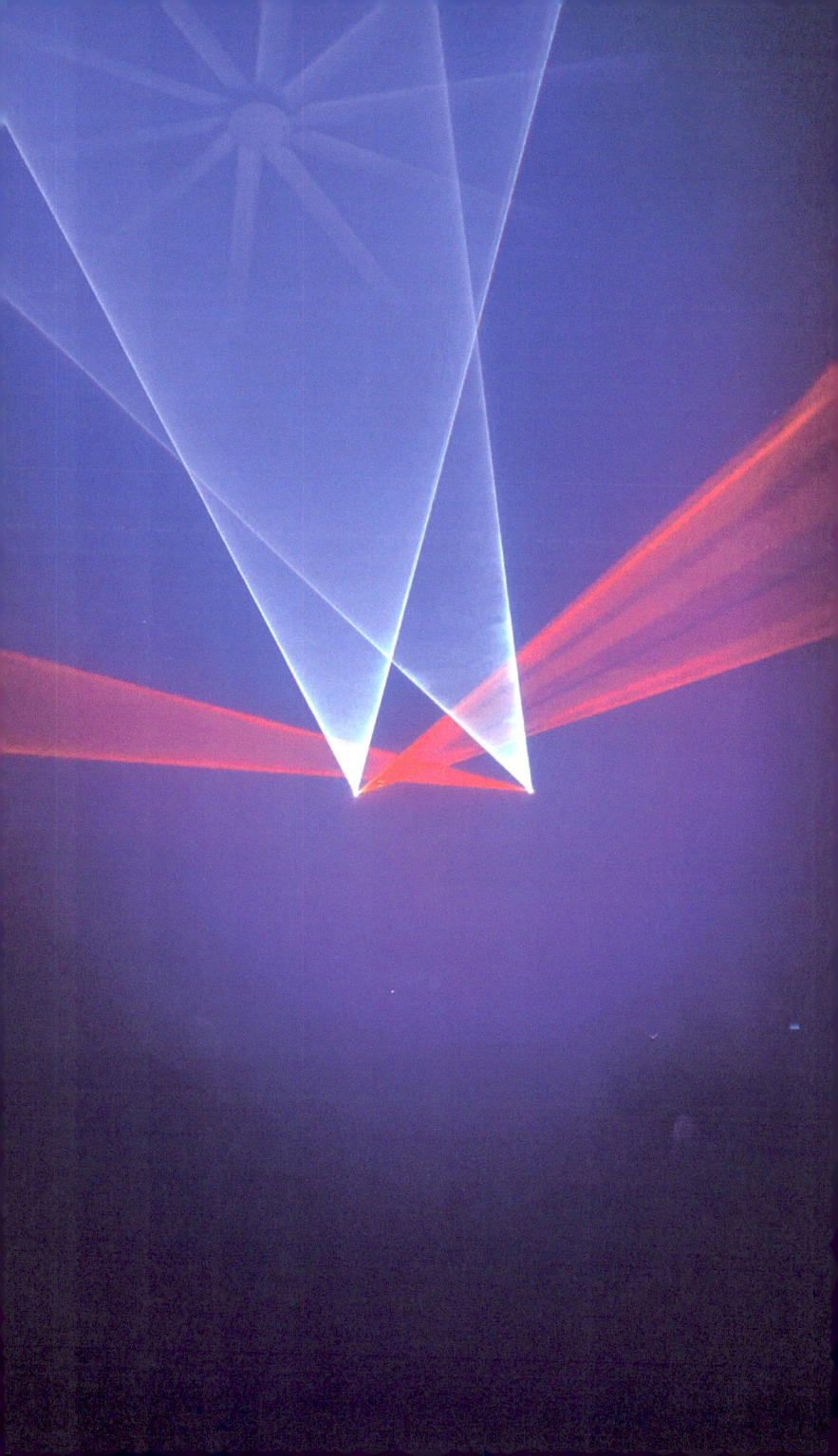

## *The Curse of a Woman*
Alfred Torres

She is a curse that seems to have no end in sight and she represents everything that I long for.
Time is merely a fallacy.
Even though it has been an eternity, I can never forget her warm embrace, her bewildering kiss.
No distance is sufficient enough to rid myself of her curse.
There is no escape.
She haunts me with her touch, her breath, and her alluring silhouette when she visits me in my dreams.
I will not hesitate to readily accept her curse with open arms the day she returns to me.
Yet, her continued torment only serves to widen the gaping void in my heart.
This is not love, it is infatuation.
Infatuated with with her every aspect, her curse: the curse of a woman.

## On a Miami Sidewalk
Neysa King

he struts past the bougainvillea
in sneakers
pink as bougainvillea

*Para Miami*

# *Welcome to Calle Ocho*
*Inna Malostovker*

# *The Beauty of Blossoming*

*Nicole Hernandez*

## *Sweater Weather*
boy blue


Florida winter doesn't like to linger
Our men are made of sand not of snow
And when it gets cold there's nowhere to go
In the town that summer calls its homestead

When the sun rests, the winter tide does its best
Clouds of cold descend onto beach homes
A film of fog glosses glass, sweats to the touch:
A bottle of gritty city left out of the fridge for the night

Warm bulbs dangle from lime palm trees,
Free of frost or snow or ice or death
As the tall stalks still hold all their leaves dear
In the season of rebirth, life holds breath here

Solstice lasts just a moment as they sleep in bundles,
Lovers huddle together under unused heaters while
Tourists brave the bars in shorts and a wife beater
Until the polar hours dwindle with the dusk...

And in a day it all goes away
A wink of winter evaporates
Into morning dew, into daylight, where
Summer moves in to make it all right again.

## *The seeds of my garden*
Shawn Cameron

Before me is my garden
Within it lies many seeds
I prance around watering them
Letting them bathe in rich sunlight
I crouch as I wait for them to grow
And yet, they never do
I begin to look around wandering
Is it the soil... too much sun... or water?
Am I to blame for their inability to flourish?
My eyes begin to wander to other gardens
Flowers blooming, free of malicious weeds
Looking with admiration from theirs to mine
I crouch once more patiently wondering
Were the seeds of my garden never meant for fruition?

## *Suddenly, a splash*

*Para Miami*

*Aleli Egües*

## *Freedom Tower*
Annie Vazquez

When they ask me where I'm from
I always say I am the daughter
of Cuban refugees.
I want people to know what runs in
my blood.

The type of stories I carry in my heart.
How I always slow down
on Biscayne Boulevard
to look at Freedom Tower.

How much this building means to me,
but how I've never had the courage
to walk inside because I am afraid to hear
the tears those walls and hallways hold.
Tiny of echoes of thousands of children
who were separated from their parents
to start an arduous journey
on their own.
Some to be reunited and others a cruel fate
to never see their loved ones again.

When they ask me where I'm from
I always say I am the daughter
of Cuban refugees.
I want people to know what liberty means,
why I love Miami, and why I
slow down to look at Freedom Tower.

### Neonic
Luis Fernando

Crystal blue beaches, city's crown
Tourists flock to soak up the sun
Vibrant culture, never dulls

## *Waiting for the bus*

*Para Miami*

*Vince Cuadra*

## *Salt in my Hair*
Cristina Menendez

Toes curled under sand
Smell of salt clears my lungs
Ocean
It beckons
To enter
Its my medicine
Waves crash over me
Healing my flesh
Deep breaths
Flowing as the current
Gently pulls
Guiding my energy in perfect harmony
Golden ball of light emerging
A new day
To Be
Now
Palm trees shaking in wind
OM
Hum of earth
Revitalize
Salt in my hair
To remember
A magical gift
Peace inside
It's all here
In this moment

## *Mimi*
Amalia Maria

Miami is where she learns to kiss at sixteen;
sucking tongues on eighth street—tippy-toeing
for rotting mouths, letting strange hands reach
underneath her salty bikini, getting caught in her
dollar store hoop earrings. Oh, Mimi—

Just another fresh-faced siren drinking tahini martinis,
turning herself into a shell :: hollowed out to hold
desires, no room for her own. An oyster girl.

She is a corpse :: tangled in egyptian cotton sheets, dissociating,
until her man for the week falls asleep to his white noise machine,
her favorite g-string stuck between his teeth. Brickell City lights fall
across his cheek.

Mimi never sleeps, only dreams. So, she grabs the hundreds from his
wallet on the nightstand and she leaves.

# *Y mira que es difícil sentir frío en Miami*
## *Jade Fernandez*

*Good morning Miami!*

*Para Miami*


*Russil Cicimbra*

# *Untitled*

*Renzo Del Castillo*

## Four Animals
Kira Rosemarie

The bay shines green like
sweet spearmint in my eyes,
cool squints against reflections
of a smooth morning surface before disrupting wakes.

Last night in moonlight, I ran
interrupted.

Pink opossum hands traipsed
over cracked cement, paw by paw,
cutting off my running path—just for a pause—
I searched for babies on her back.

She skipped like a toddler across
the road, home toward a nest
of sticks and trash and sickly-sweet
Miami gunk grown from street-gargled waste.

She was my good luck charm,
and I wished her delicate pink flesh could
replace my feet in my sneakers, carry
me wobbly over dark city terrain,

bare her teeth against the fight in the park
that I ran by next, pulling out
my phone to call police, yelling for these
man-animals to control themselves.

I stood by one fighter's wife, crying—
her left hand gripped her stroller tight and
her right wiped shocked tears.
She's pregnant, she says, that's why

She didn't jump in. She was shaking, her daughter's
eyes wide, her husband's shirt torn.
Deep breaths, I day. Do you want me
 to stay? No, she smiled.

She smiled, and I feel how strong
women are. She is above a fight—
she holds her tears, builds her baby.
I run on, thinking of opossum, fight, woman.

When I got back home, another animal
waited—a black cat, green eyes wide,
slinked away from our building. How big,
her eyes like the child's.

She crossed my path, and my mother told me the opposite.
A black cat is good luck.

This morning, bayside, cool breezes,
manatees swimming under my feet,
I still see that woman and her white grip on the stroller.
Four animals that night:

An opossum, two men, and a cat.

*Para Miami*

# La Ciudad X25
*Rafael Guillen*

### *Solitude*
*Petit Monstre*

*Para Miami*

## Subtropical Night Fever
Micah Marie Johnson


Humidity seeps from my skin
Even after midnight.

O' Miami!

I press my cheek against the window glass
To find some relief.

Melting into the night air
I become the full moon.

When you are bright in the dark
You learn to howl too.

In the city of skyscrapers endless light
I am not afraid of the night.

We are wide awake and
 Being stars won't help us sleep...

... creating new symbols of shared grief.

305:
For those who are born here.

Magic City:
For those who want it all.

South Florida:
For those who get out.

Home:

For those like me.

# *Miami at Night*

*Para Miami*

*Inna Malostovker*

## *City of dreamers*
Via Salgado

The ocean isn't the blue they try to sell you
It's the green my dad was surrounded by for weeks
The beach waves aren't big enough for surfing
But their strength rolled in my new life

The streets that raised me are ever changing
They extend like roots from a city that's grown alongside me
Bark strong enough to protect every walk of life that settles here
Different languages, foods, and cultures blossoming on its branches

The hospitality that gave my parents a job
And acceptance that never asked us to assimilate
A city filled with a different kind of dream come true
One where everyone is proof you can be anything

From doctors that offered a smile and assured my mom,
"*puedes hablar en español*"
To the grocery ladies that would trip over English to help me
I owe everything to each inch of this city
Miami, *mi ciudad*, I couldn't have asked for a better life

## *Adams Hotel (Ekphrastic)*
Renzo Del Castillo
*Inspired by "Park Avenue, 2018" from Floodzone by Anastasia Samoylova*


A stroll down cotton-candy sidewalks leads to the Adams' foyer
where a bellhop lobbies for your patronage.
It's an art deco crap-shoot;
smooth walls and sharp edges providing low relief,
a symphony of reeding and fluting filling the air with decorative span-
drels.
Here, at the Adams Hotel, they have an invariance under the transform,
an immunity to change;
a reliance on saturation and depth for impact.
The starkest of blacks and whites entwine with lavish taupes and creams
in a checkerboard motif daring you to make the first move under the
Florida sun.
You can almost ignore the potholes eroding into a moat beside the
facade
as you lean on a telephone pole, avoiding splinters while you rest.
The geometry of symmetry is exact but taste is subjective.

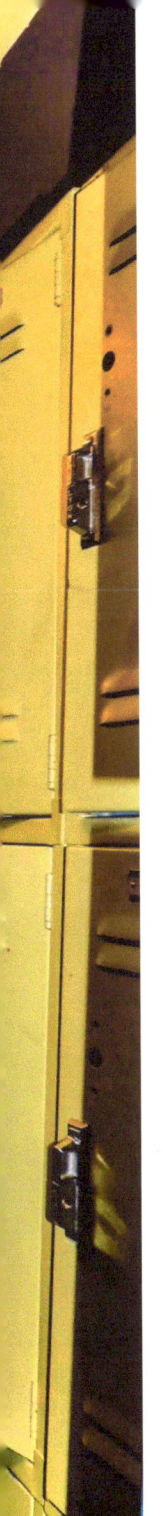

*Para Miami*

### **Untitled**
*Vince Cuadra*

# *Turquoise Sunshine*
### *Petit Monstre*

## *Showfields*
Sofia Iriarte

constellations don't matter
when it's only that one star
coloring the streets with flags
they once built with music
and coladas

pitbull, ropa vieja, and mojitos

clothing optional, lincoln road
dazing skylines, brickell casual
neon is back in space at night

laminar skies on bluer waters
bluest bliss, latina kiss
hotel room service, guest list
dreaming ultra skies, and other lies
soaked in all these blue and
other tones of la rouge


three chances
zero regret
fi(ve)nd me in miami

## *I Fell in Love in Miami and All I Got Was This Stupid Poem Out of It*
boy blue

I fell in love in Miami once. I wouldn't recommend it.
Some nights were fun and the drinks were nice, but

Don't you wonder how anyone can make a family
When we all still live with mommy and daddy?

I bloomed here, dreamed of planting my roots here,
But only the rich flowers can sign a multi-year.

A pretty little bird making minimum wage,
Smoking sage in its cage every day.

Dared to dream a little dream not grounded in reality,
Even though everyone said all we needed was a degree.

No, I've made love in Miami. It's not what you think it'd be,
Because like the beach, life gets in places you don't want to see.

Every dating app is just another voice saying I'm not enough:
Not thin, too tough, don't have fair skin, or too feminine.

Gas is high, but so am I, food's too pricy so let's just do whiskey
To forget how lame this date is, I'll find some other way to compensate.

But the rinse and repeat starts to make you feel incomplete,
Makes you wonder why do you feel the need to compete?

So please, take it from me, don't fall in love in Miami because
We're all just grown kids finding out how to be happy.

### *A call to the world above*
A.K.A

Pink, purple, and blue combined
Here, the things that you may find
Hidden in the sky's
Clouds, with ripples like waves,
Rays of light that shine
Flickering deeply in your eyes
Little sparks from up above
Singing to you with warmth or love
Always there both day and night
Never fully out of sight
It is in this place you'll see
A connection felt by you and me

## *MIA Born & Raised*
Ann DoBeDo


MIA born and raised,
That's the tagline I say,
My Chapina-American tongue,
A multicultural palate,
I ask *la visita*,
*"Que queres comer?*
*Pan con bistec, arepas, tamal, sopa de mondongo, ceviche, popusas,*
*Paella o tacos?"*
And as if the melting pot wasn't big enough I continue,
"Or we can order in, *comida China*?
There's also that new Indian place, ohhh or Jerk Chicken?"

MIA born and raised,
*Pantuflas* at home,
*Chancletas* at the beach,
*Tacones* at night.

MIA born and raised,
My number I refuse to change,
Because 786 may be Dade,
but 305... That's the way.

MIA born and raised,
My Spanglish dialect,
A harmonious weaving of,
*Vos, Dale, Yo, Bro.*

MIA born and raised,
Because we get hated on,
But if they know how we are,
*Pa' que nos invitan?*

MIA born and raised...
MIA, our magic city,
The 305,
There's nothing I would change.

## *Stolen mangoes of Miami trees*

Flor Ana

i saw a mango thief.
cherry car and cherry shirt
to camouflage.
i drove by rather quickly—
over the speed limit, but it comes to us naturally—

i know what i saw
as he stared at leaves
i have subconsciously
learned by heart,
leathered glossy and deep green.

summer season's mango thieves walk silently.
hands curled around the ripest fruit,
bent at bruises from fallen trees,
hairs rising at the backs of necks
for hairs on seeds that can be licked
avoiding the drip
of juices so sweet.

i, myself, would know,
for i, too, have stolen mangoes off Miami trees.

## *Untitled*
*Luis Fernando*

## *Water & God*
Cristina Menendez

Our higher self
Says flow
Like water
Drift with current
Instead of against
Allow energy
Through
To cleanse and nourish
Heal our wounds
Internally and externally
Connecting our
God/Goddess
Inside
Lies our balance
It's gift
For us
Is presence

# *L'amour*

*Aleli Egües*

*Memories of South Miami, 2012*

*Para Miami*

*Jade Fernandez*

## *Where I'm From*
Erin Sternstein

Where I'm from, the Torah is a metaphor for reading into each other
lives like family—born of faith, of togetherness, of same values

Where I'm from, we visit houses to pick up chocolate chip cookies,
to feast on lox and bagels, to pray

And there's a fluffy cat climbing on a washer in the laundry room

Where I'm from, my identity is wrapped around my shoulders like a
Tallit
that my grandfather placed on me on the bimah at my Bat Mitzvah

Where I'm from, we know the cantor by name
I knew his daughter once
She had brown hair and a plucky smile

Where I'm from, we bake Hamentashens in the kitchen and play a
game of witches on the playground because even though we are too
old for swings, we are never too old to use our imagination.

Where I'm from, we attend sleep away camps in North Carolina and
Birthright trips to Israel. The Lower East side is where my Bubbe was
born in 1910. She took her first steps there, just like her father when
arriving in America.

Where I'm from, my great-grandmother ran a yards good shop in
Brooklyn, and my grandfather joined the CCC, the civilian civiliza-
tion corp, at age 16 to escape Manhattan only to find that fighting
fires would not fight Anti-Semitism, and that relocating to Idaho
would become synonymous with black and blue.

Where I'm from, NYC means uptown, and Tavern on the Green

means reunion. My relatives from Yonkers, Queens, and Flatbush sit at tables and say things like "in my day," speak in Yiddish, and show me pictures of people before my time, family attending banquet halls, and Zayde in a suit with my great-great-grandfather, side by side on a street in Brooklyn where there is surely a white couple wearing tote bags pushing a stroller in front of a Whole Foods now.

Where I'm from, Boca is the last time I saw them. Zayde sitting in the back porch painting. Bubbe, with garnet nails, eating a vanilla wafer, making crumbs, washing brown glass cups. Her closet full of veiled hats, knitted shrugs.

In Deerfield Beach at Century Village, we ate chicken dinners around a table full of plastic- tablecloths, knives, and forks. In Century Village, people had numbers on their arms and Marsha, blew smoke rings out her front door. In Boca, we went to a cemetery once.

Sometimes, where I'm from feels like a distant memory.

Sometimes, I mourn it. Like an indoor plant I haven't paid much attention to in winter and its leaves turn brown in spring, wither and fall. Sometimes, we recognize
importance through absence. Sometimes, when I'm in Boca now, I close my eyes, and I can hear their voices. And I remember.

## *Heirs to the Miami Herald*
*boy blue*

*Miami's morning sky broken pier*

*Para Miami*

*Russil Cicimbra*

*Untitled*

*Para Miami*


*Vince Cuadra*

## *Sunday Service*
Annie Vazquez

On Sundays, I go to a special church in Miami.
I enter beneath orange marmalade skies
where flying seagulls sing hymns above
and sand pipers sway on the shore
like a choir to their own gospel music.
*Hallelujah, Hallelujah, Hallelujah.*
I attend sunrise service,
because it is here where I can see God.
My father taught me to choose my own religion
and find meaning in life,
but never to discuss it, or politics.
He told me about the stars and
galaxies and endless possibilities.
"You are a tiny speck in a vast universe,
learn to see beyond," he said one day
when I was crying about something trivial.
That's why I come here for sermons;
the wind, the waves, and the sun
have wisdom for me.
Nature can show us so much about life.
There is no judgment.
You can ground your feet in the sand
and find stillness.
You can close your eyes and feel the wind
instructing you on how to breathe again.
Inhale and exhale. Inhale and exhale.
You can wade in the water and into
the arms of a warm turquoise ocean
whose gentle waves hug you
while listening patiently to your
prayers and confessions,
hopes and dreams,

sadness and regrets.
You can surrender it all
without feeling like a burden.
Let go and float.
Amen.

*Para Miami*

**Untitled**
*Renzo Del Castillo*

# *Untitled*

*Luis Fernando*

## *Miami*
Alexis Basulto

We are Cuban coffee addicts, domino fanatics, flip flop walkers,
Spanish talkers, Que? You heard right, it's where English is impolite.

Pale snow birds come out to fly, enjoying our art deco sunrise.
It's where sun worshipping is a sport and everyone's in tight shorts.
If adventure is calling you, this is the place where nothing is taboo.
Peaceful Buddhists, yoga enthusiasts, inline skaters, sand joggers, hot
body builders, ocean goers, and the wave chasers, they all come out and
soak up our sun, it's like a drug and everyone wants some.

## *Depth of flow*
A.K.A

The days are long
Though full of living
The nights are strong
Built for disappearing
Where water meets land
And the tides run deep
Mysteriously there
Even while we sleep
Freeing to the touch
To those who hear the rush

## *what they don't understand*
Catalina Prieto

They tell me I deserve better
I dislike the mindset of my generation
that there's always other people out there
that if one love fails you,
another will eventually come along
But here's the thing
There will always be something better
somebody who will listen to you more
somebody who will understand you better
somebody who will show you a soft, gentle love
But that deep, human connection
you experience with that one individual
where your souls collide
and your auras intertwine
That is not something you can find in just anybody
who will simply treat you better
It's more complicated than that

*Sunset at South Pointe*

*Para Miami*

Inna Malostovker

*La Ciudad X30*

*Para Miami*

*Rafael Guillen*

## *Chanel No. 305*
boy blue

Years add change to the face of a city
Gray towers form the eyes
The graffiti is the charming history
Headlights bleed through like hair dye

Bayside could be the crown of the town
Downtown streets encircle the cheeks
In Calle Ocho, where home is found
Around Little Havana my Latin blood speaks

Coral Gables is the stuff of fables
The bushy bosom of my metropolis
Veins underground, telephone cables
Window shopping homes of the prosperous

South Miami is the heart for me
Somewhere in the lake of Tropical Park
Young cobra sneaking off to Sunset street
To see my friends or a stranger in the dark

In the stretch of the legs are other places
Like Hialeah, Miami Lakes, and Kendall
Even Wynwood has something special
For all in the state where the sun shines greatest

## Miami Is A Poem
Micah Marie Johnson


I'll take you to where
The palm trees sway.
Blue skies like sapphires—
No, like those hot gas flames.

Here, high-rises glisten
And Art Deco cracks.
The traffic weighs heavy
On the top of our backs.

I'll take you to where
The ocean meets Bae.
Party boats in the water,
Champagne's gentle spray.

Green iguanas stay relaxing,
The Groundskeepers lament
At the mess lizards make
On the pool deck's cement.

I'll take you to where
There're Murals, Graffiti and Gucci.
At brunch People ask
For a chair for their poochie.

There is chisme and language
From every corner, combined.
Pedestrians cross danger freely,
Drivers ignore all signs.

I'll take you to where
The quirks and perks are profane.

To live is to love,
To stay is insane.

A long time ago this city
Startled my soul.
There is magic in the makeup
Of these area codes.

*Para Miami*

## *Amber nights*
### *Aleli Egües*

## *Untitled*
Luis Fernando

Miami, a city of endless fun
Latino spirit, shining bold
Vibrant and colorful, our home

## Royal Palms
Renzo Del Castillo


Miami's color pastiche spreads before me,
a beach towel of polyurethane and pastels,
while the water greets hipsters and Europeans
with the warm embrace of an expectant lover.

A convention of umbrellas to my left
warns of the toll the sun will exact on my already tanned skin.
The laughter of children and remixed salsa beats intertwine,
filling the air with a mutated guaguanco
while smartphones relax for a little while
inside waterproof bags lying dormant on an ocean of sand.

Oceans join and the waves dance
with the skill of a jubilant but clumsy amateur,
white foam steps tripping over each other,
colliding with bathers,
leaving them soaked in pleasant aquamarine apologies.

An ad boat cruises by selling sunblock
as a flock of clouds gather for Sunday mass in our hot-pink
neon paradise.
May it last forever.

# *Untitled*

*Para Miami*

*Vince Cuadra*

### home was you
Catalina Prieto


Home was your arms, and the way they entangled perfectly around
my body
like the missing puzzle piece I never thought I needed
Those arms, in which made me feel safe
and where my inner child felt at ease
Home was the depth of your eyes
and the stories they told
when you looked deep within them
Home was your lips
and the way they comforted me when days felt like nothing but
torment
or the way they would wake me up in the morning
They helped me feel like the sun rays seeped through the clouds
even when it felt like the rain was never going to stop
Home was your warmth
And the way you opened your heart even when it had been taken for
granted
Home was your skin
The skin tainted by ink in which you call your temple
mesmerized by every imperfection it encompassed
It was the skin I could recognize with just the tip of my fingers
Trailing though every inch and corner
Home was no longer four walls and a ceiling

## Sun child
Via Salgado


There's an inexplicable knot in my chest
Every second my heart uncoils and the grip tightens
I laugh while voices and music surround me
But I feel nothing more than lonely
My pen runs dry from circling around my emotions
Hundreds of meaningless words dressed to look profound
Frustrated, I turn to my phone for an escape
I sink into myself for hours, feeling more ruinous
Sunlight seeps through a window and gives me light
It's burning rays graze my skin and burn me to life
I meet the heat and humidity with a slow smile
Going to meet the salty breeze, I find peace for awhile

*Para Miami*

### **Untitled**
*Renzo Del Castillo*

## *Miami is for Lovers*
Annie Vazquez

Miami is for lovers.
Maybe it's the Pisces in my Venus
or the fact that since I was 5
I live for Valentine's Day.
Red heart shaped everything and
pink notes of affection sealed
with a loud lip stained kiss.
*Muah!*
Yes, give me all the PDA.
Every day.
To feel smitten.
To have my heart jumping rope.
To dive into the arms of forever till death do us part.
I savor each second and invite it in.

In Miami, it's easy to find love.
Here, I stumble into these
get swept off your feet moments.
They come in like little thieves
and just steal my breath,
leaving me daydreaming for days.
Oh, you can find romance in every corner.
I've found it walking through Italian gardens
in Vizcaya.
People-watching at Green Street cafe.
Sitting on a blanket, sipping Merlot in a paper cup
with a Full Moon glowing in the distance
as a pianist serenades a crowd of us
from the shores of the Setai.

You should've seen the smile
on my coconut oil glazed lips

one balmy summer night.
Palm trees rustling
as a hot rain
tumbled out of the sky
at a Bayfront park concert,
baptizing hundreds of bodies.
My body.
Our wet skins glistening with the stars
as we swayed to the
music.

I've tasted love on my lips in Calle Ocho
and never forgotten it.
*Fruta bomba* milkshakes and *cafecitos*.
*Croquetas* and *pastelitos de guava*.
And if I still haven't convinced you,
go pick giant juicy strawberries amongst
a field of towering sunflowers with dancing bees
at a U Pick in Kendall.
Or head up to find the Rainbow Eucalyptus tree
at Fairchild,
whose bark looks like
it was hand painted with splashes
of green, blue, and orange.
You'll then know why
Miami is for lovers.

## *Potential Energy*
Renzo Del Castillo


The waters absorb the light, drowning
the shore strewn with garbage. A heron uses
an MGD bottle to triangulate its position
for a landing. It stares at the turtles from a grassy perch,
high as the walls of Troy.
The colors are ill-suited for mid-afternoon.
Too many egrets occupy the right side of the sky.
O Lake, you lack the nuance of a master's brush.
The egrets, off-white and refusing to hold their poses,
flap like forgotten pamphlets.
The herons have taken flight, the egrets as well, leaving the matted
grass.
Some tan-faced men picked up the MGD bottle,
perhaps to be recycled. Mosquitoes fill the air.
Even the sunlight has left the waters.

## Sundays are for Brunch
Flor Ana

we live in a city where everything is
garnished with *maduros* or mojitos.
where the music lives on every street corner,
ranging from rock to *reggaeton*.

we live for the art scene and we love to
flaunt our sun-kissed bodies under evergreen suns.
we play with the waves that come and wash away
various news of "florida man..." and "florida woman..."

we live in a city that sleeps in on mondays
because sundays are for brunch
and we're all in need of a bloody mary
or champagne-with-a-splash-of-orange-juice mimosa.

we live for the experience,
the never ending *cancioncitas* and dance,
and i hope that, if you find yourself here, living like the rest of us,
you'll close your eyes and smile, and take the world by chance.

## *Paradise on earth*
Rū

In a light blue background,
Resting its majestic shine over a lilac blanket,
The sun pounders over Miami.
With its golden touch,
The city glistens and the palm trees dance in awe of the breeze.
The orange juice is fresh,
The girls are pretty, and the music is blasting.
Beaches are vibrant, inevitable smiles, and a true Eden
Here on earth.
While we enjoy this paradise,
The world can only dream of it.

*Para Miami*

*The Artists*

**A.K.A.** is a Miami-based poet who finds inspiration in nature. Her flourishing curiosity in the metaphysical world began at a young age when she discovered and indebted herself to the Wiccan religion. The deep connection she feels toward the divine universe has driven her to dedicate her life to esoteric teachings, such as tarot card reading, energy healing, and spiritual guidance. A.K.A. uses her relationship with nature to create thought-provoking poems that invoke an emotional link between the natural and spiritual worlds. Her poetry can also be viewed in *The Spell Jar: Poetry for the Modern Witch.*
*Connect with A.K.A on Instagram: @dappy_doe*

**Flor Ana** is a Cuban-American writer, poet, and musician who made her literary debut with her self-published poetry collection, *Perspective (and other poems)*, which went on to become a bestseller at Barnes & Noble locations across South Florida. Since her literary debut, Flor has released various poetry collections, including *The Language of Fungi & Flowers, Nourish Your Temple: Self-Love & Care Poetry,* and *A Moth Fell In Love With The Moon. Connect with Flor on Instagram: @littleearthflower*

**boy blue** is a Florida native born and raised in Miami for over 20 years before starting his education at Tallahassee Community College, currently studying creative writing and film at the University of Central Florida in Orlando pursuing a future in media writing. boy blue self-published his first poetry book, *boys.* in college during the pandemic lockdown in 2020, featuring his own photography and illustrations. Shortly after, he released his second collection *This Vicious Cycle* in 2022.
*Connect with boy blue on Instagram: @byboyblue*

**Russil D. Cicimbra, also know as Rū,** is a Miami-based, Venezuelan-born photographer, poet, and medical technologist. A Miami Fair and Expo winner, Rū learned photography at the age of fifteen. After she developed her first film photos, she knew that she would not let go of this craft. Now, she has transferred her film eye in to the digital eye realm, exhibiting her work overseas in Montreal, Canada in August of 2022 at GORA Gallery, as well as in Minneapolis, Minnesota at Praxis Gallery,

Bridgeport Art Center in Chicago, Illinois, THE SPACE Art Gallery in Philadelphia, Pennsylvania, FotoZA Gallery in Johannesburg, South Africa, Valid World Hall Gallery in Barcelona, Spain, and Sparks Gallery in San Diego, California. Winning contests through GuruShots, Rū has also been featured in the amateur photographer magazine *Doho*.
*Connect with Rū on Instagram: @russilc*

**Vince Cuadra** is a 19-year-old queer-trans Costa Rican-Argentinian multimedia artist born and raised in Miami, Florida. Vince's work is very playful, colorful and heavily inspired by his Miami upbringing and nostalgia. He started taking photography more seriously at the age of 13 documenting anything and everything that he found interesting on a handheld digital camera and fell in love with street photography and spontaneous photo taking. Ever since he's continued to do a lot of in the moment photography, mostly capturing the streets, architecture, events, and people of Miami as well as places he may travel.
*Connect with Vince on Instagram: @goblin157*

**Renzo Del Castillo** was born in Lima, Peru, immigrating to the US when he was 5 years old. Renzo graduated from the University of Florida with a B.A. in English, specializing in Victorian Literature, and an M.A. in Mass Communications, specializing in Intercultural Communications. While he has spent the last 10 years as an executive in the healthcare industry, Renzo is a poet and has been published in Literary Yard, the Acentos Review, the Scarlet Leaf Review, and the Ekphrastic Review.
*Connect with Renzo on Instagram: @elrenz.*

**Ann DoBeDo** is an optimist with an evolutionary approach to life. Ann derives from personal experiences, interactions with others, and her own imaginative thoughts to create pieces that she hopes will inspire and touch the lives of other humans. With every word chosen, she intertwines emotions and everyday experiences in hopes of inciting new dialogue that will lead to positive change.
*Connect with Ann on Instagram: @anndobedo*

**Aleli Egües** is a Miami based artist whose practice deals with vintage references and the relationship between the landscape and the feminine. She works in photography, video, video-based performance and expanded painting. Aleli's artwork has been featured at SCOPE Miami International Art Fair, Doral Contemporary Art Museum (DORCAM), Miami Art Week, The Nightclub, the South Florida Latin American Photography Forum amongst others. According to Aleli, "Photography, video, and expanded painting are my canvas for exploring female identity, the landscape, and performance art. My work is campy and poetic, beautifying the daily and mundane. Synchronicities between people and nature, space and time interest me; I feel that everything is interconnected."
*Connect with Aleli on Instagram: @aleliart*

**Jade Fernandez** was born and raised in Miami and currently lives in New York. Photography has alway felt like a visual book she was slowly writing, and when she started, all she wanted to do was tell stories about her life through her photographs. Jade studied at Parsons School of Design for Photography and Eugene Lang School of Liberal Arts for Literary Studies with a double concentration in Journalism and Creative writing. Narrative has always been important to her, which makes her the perfect photographer to tell your story because that is what she cares about the most. The passion in her work comes from getting to know different individuals and focusing on the ability to create portraits with respectful and creative representation. The people who book her seek to have genuine moments captured and let their imagination inspire them.
*Connect with Jade on Instagram: @lo.lace.love*

**Rafael Guillen** is a Venezuelan photographer and audiovisual producer. He studied arts and cinema at the Central University of Venezuela and has participated in a number of individual and collective exhibitions in Mexico, Venezuela, and Panama, including FotoSeptiembre 2003 with his series "Sangre, Sudor y Lágrimas" and the French Alliance of Panama with his series "La luz y la ciudad" in 2019. In addition to making productions audiovisuals for the Articruz workshop with Carlos Cruz-Diez, Rafael has worked on series such as "Panamá es Negro y Blanco," "Conocidos/Des-

conocidos," and even made a TV series called "Rutas y Colores de Panamá." Recently, Rafael has worked his series "Ciudad de los semáforos infinitos" and "La Ciudad X," which is showcased in this anthology. The focus of Rafael's work seeks angles out of the ordinary, far from the perspective of classic cannons. In 2022, Rafael exhibited in New York at the Latin American Art Triennial, representing Venezuela in the celebration of Hispanic Heritage.
*Connect with Rafael on Instagram: @rafaelguillen*

**Nicole Hernandez, also known as the Calm Cuban,** was born and raised in Miami, FL. She invests her time teaching mindful movement and meditation, and jokingly says, "If I can be calm, anyone can." Her struggles with anxiety inspired her to become a mental health advocate and she's on a mission to help humans feel less alone and more connected, with themselves and others. Photography and writing are meditative experiences for her as much as forms of creative self-expression. She took a special liking to nature photography as it helps her practice mindfulness and gratitude while connecting to the natural world. Since the age of 9, she's loved taking photos. As her cameras evolved from a Polaroid, Nikon, to an iPhone, one thing remains the same—the joy of capturing beauty through the lens of her eyes.
*Connect with Nicole on Instagram: @calmcuban*

**Sofia Iriarte** is a Barcelona-born poet and author who migrated to the Florida at the age of 16 and is studying Communications at Florida International University. Sofia made her literary debut at the age of 12 with her poem "El Jardí De La Vida," which was published in a magazine in Barcelona. Her work has also been featured in The Spell Jar: Poetry for the Modern Witch. Sofia thrives off cryptic wording and metaphors to express herself in her poetry and never fully knows what's on her mind. Her debut poetry collection, Bravery, Heart & Red Shoes, which details Sofia's coming of age journey from Spain to the US and her feelings throughout released in 2022.
*Connect with Sofia on Instagram: @siriartte*

**Micah Marie Johnson** is an upbeat artist and writer know for their introspective poetry that often take a humorous turn and explores an eclectic landscape. As a vibrant community builder, Micah has joined the leadership of nonprofit Miami Poetry Club as their Director of Development on their mission to help writers write! Micah's writing has appeared in a poetry and short story anthology titled *Journey's End* by Two Friends Publishing , as well as in SWIIM's collaboration with FIU's Wolfsonian Public Humanities Lab (WPHL) and FIU's Center for Women's and Gender Studies, called Sing The Body. Micah has also been a featured poet in O'Miami Poetry events during National Poetry Month. Their first children's book, *Finding The Future*, is a commissioned project to commemorate the opening of the library of the future, The Cybrarium Library in Homestead, Florida.
*Connect with Micah on Instagram: @thecuriousmicah*

**Neysa King**'s writing has been featured by O Miami, Bread Loaf Writers' Conference, Community of Writers, Sand Berlin Literary Journal, Darling Magazine, SWWIM Every Day, and others. She is the author of two poetry chapbooks, *Rainbow Body* (2021) and *My Heart Points Back* (2022). She is the co-founder and executive director of Miami Poetry Club (@miamipoetryclub), a nonprofit dedicated to helping Miami writers improve their craft. She lives in Miami Beach.
*Connect with Neysa on Instagram: @neysaking*

**Inna Malostovker** is a nature and fine art photographer and digital photo artist. Born in St. Petersburg, Russia, Inna made her way to the Sunshine State by way of downtown Manhattan and the North Carolina foothills and now works out of Miami, Florida. When she won her very first camera in a traffic safety competition held by a local newspaper at the age of twelve, a bonus prize lifelong passion arrived with it. Though rooted in a dedicated mission to explore all technical aspects of photography as a craft, Inna's true satisfaction still comes from clambering through the mud or perching on a narrow ledge to capture that perfect shot. A joy matched only by the ability to share these unique perspectives with others, whether it is through the capture of landscapes or macro shots, wildlife images or

abstract compositions.
*Connect with Inna on Instagram: @inna_malostovker*

**Amalia Maria** is a poet and creative nonfiction writer from Miami, Florida and is currently pursuing her B.A in Creative Writing from the University of Central Florida. Amalia's writing ranges from intimate poetry to nonfiction essays, written creatively using techniques from writing workshops. Her work has been featured in *The Spell Jar: Poetry for the Modern Witch.*
*Connect with Amalia on Instagram: @amaliamariaps*

**Cristina Menendez** is an artist who studied theatre and motion pictures at the University of Miami. She realized acting was an outlet for all her pent up emotions that societal conventions kept her from expressing. She then transitioned into marketing with the notion of working for famous celebrities and/or luxury brands. Cristina built up an extensive resume working for brands like MTV, Sony LATAM, Disney, Saks Fifth Avenue and Burberry. The reality was each role she took on pulled her further down the rabbit hole of disempowerment. The universe heard her plea and threw motherhood into her mix. When Cristina's first child was two, she began reading about teaching children emotional intelligence. This resonated within her deeply and she became a Reiki Master, Medical Intuitive, Light Language Channeler and Sound Bowl Player. She studied the Tarot and is a Soul Teacher from Nikki Novo's Soul Collective. She went back to her writing roots from her high school years, where she was Editor and Chief of the school's literary magazine. Cristina began writing again, and she is currently working on a screenplay geared towards teenagers with a key message: embracing their differences. Cristina now offers to guide people to their own purpose and knowing through Energetic Activations. She helps others remember that they are infinite beings having a human experience. She guides her clients in remembering their own gifts and powers. She brings their attention to the present moment so they can observe their own self-talk. Cristina is a guided/intuitive, light worker here to help you remember your light.
*Connect with Cristina on Instagram: @cristyhappyplace*

**Catalina Prieto** was born and raised in Miami, Florida, and is currently 19-years-old attending Florida International University, with dreams of immersing herself into the creative and artistic realm. A self-taught poet, Catalina draws inspiration from other authors and is driven to compose and publish her own poetry collection on topics including mental health, relationships, and more. In Catalina's opinion, writing is the most authentic form of self-expression as it offers audiences a place to read and feel understood. Writing gives Catalina the opportunity to delve deeply into her thoughts and communicate her perspectives on life to the rest of the world.
*Connect with Catalina on Instagram: @caticasworld*

**Kira Rosemarie** is a writer and artist from Kentucky, currently living in South Florida. She writes short fiction and poetry, and has had works published in Sad Girls Club Literary Blog, The Dillydoun Review, and Cathexis Northwest Press. Her debut chapbook, *Moon/Season*, released in 2022 with Bottlecap Press.
*Connect with Kira on Instagram: @busy_witch*

**Viamelys Salgado, known to most as Via Salgado,** is a Cuban-born and Miami-raised student at Florida International University for biology. She plans to pursue veterinary science in school while striving to achieve her life-long dream of authorship outside of it. Reading and writing for as long as memory serves, poetry came relatively late from poetry grew to love, and only a few years later, she started to compete in it. With some awards at the state high-school level and writing experience in more journalistic pursuits, she's excited to see and share wherever the world of words takes her next. *Connect with Via on Instagram: @via.13_*

**Erin Sternstein** is a poet, playwright, yoga teacher and teaching artist whose work focuses on disrupting rape culture, uplifting survivor's of gender based violence, and normalizing conversations around mental health. In 2017, she developed a comedic one-woman show, *#MeToo*, at

the Marsh Theatre in San Francisco under the guidance of director David Ford, which had its world premiere at the largest solo theatre festival on the West Coast, The Whitefire Theatre's SOLOFEST. The show then went on to perform at The Hollywood Fringe Festival in 2018 and Second City Hollywood in 2019. Erin is a former member of the Oakland Slam Poetry Team and has read and performed poetry at La Mama Galleria, Queensfest at the Odyssey Theatre, The Bootleg Theater, The Pussy Powerhouse in Los Angeles, and most recently performed at Governor's Island at the NYC Poetry Festival. Her poetry was accepted into the 2021 Every Woman Biennial Festival and showcased as an NFT at the Superchief NFT Gallery. Her poem "And so it is" was published by Sagewoman Magazine in 2016, and she self-published a small chapbook in 2018 entitled *Your Pussy is Magic*. Erin's writing has appeared in publications such as BUST Magazine and Shakti Yogi Journal, and her play was accepted into the NYC 1 Minute Play Festival in 2020. In 2022, she partnered with the NYC Mayor's Office to ENDGBV and was the host of VOICES: Survivor's Speak- an evening of healing and transforming through the arts in collaboration with ArtTransforms.
*Connect with Erin on TikTok: @eldermillenial86*

**Annie Vazquez** is a poet, writer, and former freelance journalist featured in the Miami Herald, Refinery29, NBC6, and Vogue. Her blog, The Fashion Poet, is Miami's #1 lifestyle blog and her wellness brand, Annie the Alchemist, has been featured on People Magazine, Man Repellar, and Time Out Magazine. Annie has published ebooks on self-love and wellness, has released an affirmation deck titled *Affirmations for Abundance*, and has been featured in *The Spell Jar: Poetry for the Modern Witch*.
*Connect with Annie on Instagram: @anniewriteswords*

## *ABOUT THE PUBLISHER*

# INDIE EARTH
PUBLISHING

Indie Earth Publishing is an independent,
author-first co-publishing company based in Miami, FL, dedicated to
giving writers the creative freedom they deserve when publishing their
poetry, fiction, and short story collections. Indie Earth provides its
authors a plethora of services meant to aid them in their book publishing
experiences and finally feel they are releasing the book of their dreams.

With Indie Earth Publishing, you are more than just an author, you are
part of the Indie Earth creative family, making a difference one book at a
time.

www.indieearthbooks.com

For inquiries, please email:
indieearthpublishinghouse@gmail.com

Instagram: @indieearthbooks